"Surrealism is based on the belief
in the omnipotence of dreams,
in the undirected play of thought."

— Andre Breton (1896-1966)

Also by Fabrice Poussin

In Absentia (Silver Bow Publishing 2021)
If I Had A Gun (Silver Bow Publishing 2022)

HALF PAST LIFE

by

Fabrice Poussin

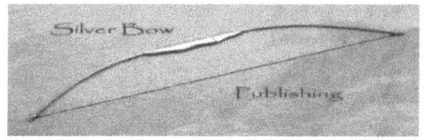

Silver Bow Publishing
720 Sixth Street, Box # 5
New Westminster, BC
CANADA   V3L3C5

Title: Half Past Life
Author: Fabrice Poussin
Cover Photo: "Heaven's Gate" by Fabrice Poussin
Layout and Editing: Candice James
ISBN: 9781774032619(print)
ISBN: 9781774032626 (e-book)

All rights reserved including the right to reproduce or translate this book or any portions thereof, in any form except for the use of short passages for review purposes, no part of this book may be reproduced, in part or in whole, or transmitted in any form or by any means, electronically or mechanically, including photocopying, recording, or any information or storage retrieval system without prior permission in writing from the publisher or a license from the Canadian Copyright Collective Agency (Access Copyright)

ISBN: 9781774032619 Print
ISBN: 9781774032626 eBook
© 2023 Silver Bow Publishing

Library and Archives Canada Cataloguing in Publication

Title: Half past life / by Fabrice Poussin.
Names: Poussin, Fabrice, author.
Description: Poems.
Identifiers: Canadiana (print) 2023045819X | Canadiana (ebook) 20230458211 | ISBN 9781774032619 (softcover) | ISBN 9781774032626 (Kindle)
Classification: LCC PS3616.O875 H35 2022 | DDC 811/.6—dc23

"To my sister Betty and her husband Bernard, whose support is unprecedented, even as they go through their own personal hardships."

Contents

A Bigger Man Than She / 9
A Dog's Life / 10
A Droplet Ago /11
A Little Piece Of Heaven / 12
A Perfect Death / 13
A Plea In The Desert / 14
A Visit Home / 15
A World Apart / 16
Aces Up / 17
Alchemy / 18
… And He Was Gone / 20
Another Dead Letter In Space / 21
Anticipation / 22
Anxious Words / 23
Benches / 25
Blonde In The Park / 26
Blood Of Ice / 27
Born At Last / 28
Brain / 29
Breaking Another World / 30
Building A Wave / 31
Color Of Her Pain / 32
Custom Made / 33
Dreaming A Destiny / 34
Eternal Thread / 35
Final Leap / 36
Flight Of The Hours / 37
Forever Ago / 38
Gusts / 39
Half Past Life / 40
Harvesting A Noble Death / 41
His Daddy's Old Mirror / 42
Hissing Man / 43
Holiday / 44
How About The Seasons / 45
How Many Times / 46
I, The Madwoman / 47
If / 48
In Black And White / 49
In Search Of The Word / 50

Jolly Monsters / 51
Just Like The Old Poet / 52
Keep The Door Ajar / 53
Larry / 54
Last Drink / 55
Left Behind / 56
Letter to My Brain / 57
Limbs And More / 59
Listen To The World Cry / 60
Long Beards And Fat Bellies / 61
Loud Secrets / 62
Macaroni And Apple Sauce / 63
Making Your Dream / 64
Meaning / 65
Memories For The Otherworld / 66
Missing / 67
Mother / 68
My Girl / 69
My Midas / 70
My Rolls And I / 71
Never Too Late / 72
Nice Piece Of Living / 73
No More Decembers / 74
The Death Of Summer / 75
Trashing The World / 76
If This Is Where God Lives... / 77
$200 A Night / 78
In The Ivory Tower / 80
Old West Glories / 81
If The Noise Could Cease / 82
Spitting In The Grass / 83
The Proposal / 84

A Bigger Man Than She

Standing tall beneath the rocky peaks
she towers in a world of ruthless power
devoid of noble care.

Errors in fibs lie at the feet of her prey
with a choice to hide under an Eve's cave
or to burn in the heat of certain pain.

Caught in a trap of her own making she shivers
to soon omit a vague memory and
return to her reading.

Asking for forgiveness she sleeps in peace.
It seems chapters have already passed
as she smiles.

It takes a bigger man than she to grant her wish.
Crushed under the cruel heels of eternal aloofness
she laughs and all is well.

A Dog's Life

I do remember the dog days of summer
when it seems I had more time to run,
play outside, chase squirrels and cardinals.

There was a ritual I never understood
when I found myself alone in the garage
suddenly empty of the twin automobiles.

I heard a commotion of words and motion
of course, you may say I cannot be sure
since my language is of images alone.

I do think I began to grasp the concepts
as they looked at their wrists, a clock on a wall
and a well-dressed woman on TV, seeking advice.

It was always the same refrain
as they spoke of meetings, appointments
and the rigors of what they called daily schedules.

I have stored these flashes of their lives in my memories
elements of the puzzle that tell their stories
of a mad race through very strange lives.

So, I stayed on my little bed set on the grey concrete
alone surrounded by the tools of other moments
when they stayed and busied themselves at home.

Quite unaware of their activities I slept
only to hear the lovely sound of an opening door
as if it had been just an instant since they left.

Yet the song began again, and I grew tired of
the complaints, concerns, and affirmations;
so many things must be done before they leave again.

Then I heard the calling of my room
and I decided it was best to make myself scarce
as a storm was forming in those impossible lives.

A Droplet Ago

She remembers
atop Everest, she came to life
so round, so shiny, transparent, and perfect
but then she fell and rolled and rolled again.

It was a long way to the stream, torrent, river
but sweet as she was, she made it to her dear sea
in a bathing suit made of light from a sun and distant stars.

No one remembers the name given to her by the firmament
it has been centuries yet until she awoke again
at the foot of a golden goddess of blue diamonds
and silky robes in sweetest morning dew.

She remembers
in the vast ocean, her soul burning
a vision of a breast giving life in kind embrace
and, at last, the glimpse of a son upon a faraway nebula.

She smiled once, perhaps it was a grin of pain
as she fell from the ragged cliffs above.

No one remembers the name of the apparition in our hopes.
She, too, dreamed of a friend below the clouds
lost in an immensity of giants
no one in fact noticed.

She cried, my dear, she screamed and she died on the rock,
shattered like ancient stone upon the abyss
then she fell, into the deep,
quiet, gentle, making a night.

She had a name.
Mistress of lands beyond.
She was the domain of her births.

A Little Piece Of Heaven

Late by the dimming spark of an abandoned candle
she stumbled upon pieces of other people's memories
buried deep at the foot of her forgotten attic
celebrated by shrouds of ancestral dust.

Soon she found herself outside of time
sitting in her little girl's summer dress
as she might in a formal gown to an ancient ball
entering a palace made for glorious damsels.

Before her, old postcards bearing secret codes
encyclopedias to the dearly departed
her soul begins to smile as she understands
connections to those who made her world.

A postmark from another continent
ominous years when humanity collapsed
wounds transported across oceans
to the quiet hearth of her young refuge.

Letters preciously preserved within beds
of pastel sheets dormant for decades
speak to her in the tongue of dreams
warm with the sounds of a long dynasty.

Pioneers, and warriors, lost migrants on a terrifying island
she hears the pitches of their words, laughter, and tears
alive in the little paradise she made
the voice of Heaven surrounds her.

A Perfect Death

There is no sweeter sense of a daze
than the glimmering edge of the sword
resting on your palm.

Joy permeates through your gaze
for you know the depth of your intent
clear in your breast.

Standing as if in an antique duel
in a stance not unlike that of a fierce tango
you may strike at will while you smile.

The point will cause no pain
a quick arrow to vital powers
yet slow for a thoughtful thrust.

I await the parting of the vermillion fibers
upon the cold steel of a bluish blade
carving a path to the awe of the abyss.

Then two warmths united by the flow of life
glad as they see the eyes of sleep
gently closing onto a most intimate numbness.

Her fingers now limp let loose of the handle
as the blood flows to the entrails of their soil
and a gentle kiss joins their fleeting lips.

A Plea In The Desert

It is in an unexpected genuflection
in a desert land devoid of movement
where this wanderer has come to rest.

It may be the end of the long journey
grasping at fantasies in this fiery furnace
under a threatening oblivion of darkness.

Rusty, ruby-red rocks cut at his tired limbs
into what was once the robust copy of a giant
now taking bashful breaths of a life no longer his.

Covered in hesitating veins like bursting blue decay
he looks up to a gentler realm beyond the storm
his heart still, already deep inside the hollow prison.

He recalls holding the vanishing flake
believing his passion could give it permanence
as if an alchemist he could make ice from a flame.

One final flash of a trek to the rainy marble temple
to touch the perfect form of a godly shape
the memory of yesterday is so long entombed.

The world barren to him now, safe perhaps
for the in-print of a tear he cannot restrain
to cross millennia, a reminder of an extinct species.

His hands to the furious winds, it is his last attempt
to form, to hold, and to save within his pleading palms
the little soul who never so much as heard his sighs.

A Visit Home

He recalls the days when he ruled over the landscape
terrorizing his seniors with his silly pranks;
famous across the land for his noble deeds
as he grew to respect the wishes of the elders.

Acquaintances vanished before their day
friends too went their early way to the grave
surrounded by those who brought them to this place;
their names now carved in frigid stone.

It still rains in spring as in his memories
the sun continues to scorch the earth in August
a constant with the strangers who now live there
upon the earth where he no longer belongs.

Walls remember his cries, the soil his falls.
Trees bear the scars of his many escapades
when he played at war with his gang
and greeted the whole village on his way to school.

His palaces will stand on the hill for centuries
homes to unfamiliar glances sealed to the visitor
now unwelcome in the world that gave him life
patiently awaiting his boyish adventures.

Why does he not visit more often they ask
his answer simple as he stares at the surroundings
the lifeline has been severed for too long
and fences built around the trees he loved.

A World Apart

Only A few feet above the sea
a bridge through the strange spaces
of those who never truly die.

A road flows on through villages
ran down by too many sorrows
wooden shacks creek in enduring agony.

The radio attempts to utter one last tune
along with the humming of soft concrete
like a funeral march under the cypress trees.

Streets lined with dying dreams of white picket fences
eyes onto those forgotten souls droop in rotten frames
hanging by the rusty thread of crying hinges.

At dawn the mist whimpers in heavy loneliness
at noon an eerie smoke hovers from cabin to mansion
dusk only brings the rest they so sorely need.

We continue the eternal journey through this wasteland
quiet as the aftermath of great battles
abandoned even by those who still live.

Aces Up

The cards spread on the crumbling table
oddly lined and stacked in a child's game
the tin box of goodies and sweets at hand's reach
she coughs and grabs the snuff predictably.

Time has stopped for her, she has no more
of a need for it than she would a tank or a sword
a great partner at play with the bribe, as always
her heart gallops with a known excitement.

Little Legs came from another country it seems
though in summer every day, at the same time
he makes his appointment with the lady
wrinkly, who sometimes still gardens a little.

No pets around, but the old TV set seems to meow
bark, buzz with lives hunched over, by the hearth
she wipes her nose nonchalantly, adjusting her glasses
it is already the third hand and she is points behind.

The sun lingers, thinking of a short night ahead
ripening wheat, corn, and grapes, bored yet faithful;
the lady has little care for much anymore
the hands on the clock have fallen with the last news.

An accident, a calamity, a storm, a war, a few gunshots,
hunting season again, is it? Ah, she might kill indeed
for the taste of the latest vine of her fields forgotten
no longer harvester, like the child she once was, she plays.

Alchemy

An alchemist unaware, you are filled
with the tricks of millennia of magic,
your wand is your desire etched
in your eyes, a future spreading
through dimensions of time.

You pose in silence, protected by
the solitude you seem to cherish.

Surrounded by a semi-darkness, you shape,
you master the world in infinitesimal
portions; your being sublime.

Still, a silhouette against the glass frame,
dark ocean of your ebony curls.

Maker of miracles, in the private alcove
you are owner of the pulses which
make all things begin their motion.

It begins deep inside, in a tickle, a soft
jolt, an explosion unexplained, and
you smile, as whole, you can taste
a transformation, almost a kick.

Acrobat without safety, motionless,
your life under the big top, all in glory,
trapped by the shock of the clown,
a lion's roar, the unlikely dancing cats
your eyes slowly metamorphose.

Quietly, in complete contemplation,
slipping into unconsciousness it seems,
your strength grows inward a little,
of so many more lives liberated.

Powerless, the spectator can only fathom

your act made of all talents combined
hoping for your gaze, reassuring
that he too may become part
of your experiment
as you open your eyes again
and give him a smile.

You are the great alchemist
granter of wishes,
you alone, remember,
can set him free
in your solid embrace.

...And He Was Gone

Dwelling on the scraps of despair
counting the blessings in greasy wrap
he waited for the opportune hour
to begin another cycle with this world.

'Twas eight before horns clamored again
pearls of mist adorned his shaggy faded locks;
was there room at all for a slight dream
behind these eyes blind to compassion?

Upon vespers, he stood by the concrete pillars
folding an invisible robe of Hermine and gold
he confused the torn plaid of a found coat
for the fleece of the realm's emperor.

He greeted those who passed by in their carriages
words lost to the turbulence of mechanical winds
the drivers barely saw this semblance of a man
thin with the hunger of a thousand years.

And then it was twilight on a Saturday eve
many stood at attention before the scene
upon the embankment, bleachers to the theater
for the first time a great audience beneath a show of lights.

Not one could pass the road any longer
as humanoid shapes were busy with the task
behind the black and whites of the cruisers
the fire engines and emergency transports.

It has been weeks since the road was blocked
now the grass is quiet under the concrete shade
there is no need to slow one's pace anymore
for he has gone if he ever was.

Another Dead Letter In Space

Throwing letters at the depth of space
as if it were Morse code or a strange cipher
I continued imagining they were boomerangs
and would return to me with a secret missive.

Grammar was not a main concern nor commas
perhaps my words did not come to life of their own
but I hoped a nurturing soul would capture
the unformed syllables and fashion them to a thought.

Upon the wall of infinity, I wished for an echo
a vibration to endure until it touched the membrane
of a mate entangled in a domain invisible
safe from this world, living in ecstasy.

All mighty in the isolation I had so chosen
lord of the city deserted of all life
I extended those hopeful arms submitted
to the shattering response from another realm.

The letter would remain dead to this earth
yet I know the universe took notice
preserving my message across the dimensions
and in a place unknown it was known in whole.

Anticipation

Little golden top hovers
a tiny nose reaches for the scent
of the sweet ingredients married by her hands
as she labors tenderly for the dominical feast.

He may not notice the dot of a white powder
though it teases the nubile skin of ten
digits keeping his uncertain balance
upon the edge of an antique marble.

She means to ignore him as she kneads
but her heart hugs his fancies so mightily
he smiles at the touch of her nurturing breast
in the silence of a breath he knows so well.

The dough color of a hazy sunset
comes alive with the life of a mother
he can already smell the baking of Sunday
so many delights his soul has tasted.

Now he is still, she dares gaze at the rascal
she stops everything to inhale and to smile
feeding the complicity only they know
by the hearth they freeze in an eternal masterpiece.

Anxious Words

Forgotten on the wobbly table,
the letter lies silent,
smeared by a drop,
rain or tear.

Deserted, the chair calls his name,
to return and complete
with a syllable or two,
the love just begun.

Through the window the crops,
and beyond, hues of orange
and red say good night
yet it is not time.

The floor speaks in high pitches,
one time, twice, and again,
a shadow looms over the paper,
responding to the unspoken.

No longer alone the chair swivels,
an instant blinded by the setting day,
the warmth of eve shoots
straight to his heart.

From the soul, the ink will flow,
to fulfill what is yet unresolved,
one last line of China ink,
married to soft velum.

And perhaps another wet dot,
his lips twitching in a smile,
his body uplifted in sweet passion,
alive as he draws the world.

For his hands are done,
his feet will rest into infinite sleep,
surrounded by the reigning
light over all dark things.

The fire has died down for now,
the world's syllables are still
yet he remains, undisturbed,
the last tear finally frozen.

Benches

Cold as ice in the deep of a winter night
concrete and rebar make up the cozy bed
to lovers in search of a forgotten home.

Shining with the showers of a breezy March
metal as lace impossible for a brief rest
with only memories of a dying Valentine.

Into antique days of primal artists
as if the flesh of naked Adam and Eve alone
marbled by the weary stance at battle.

Knight for his lady under the shade
in a fortress of century oaks, he builds a shack
armor to silk tunic to travel to Avalon as one.

Now among the fields of red clay and fashioned greens
molded by the white safety of science, they melt
in an August heat abandoned for the false safety of distance.

Resting upon the clouds of heaven, ancestors ponder
lines of Sappho, Petrarch, and William with a sigh
for the moments too ephemeral vanished into eternity.

What has happened to the quiet locus they sought
makeshift benches, masterpieces molded by fiery passions?
It is time to leave the tower filled with the sorrows of winter.

Blonde In The Park

Is it the sun she seeks in the lonely hour
the quietude of a deserted park
when everything seems to hibernate
for balmy summer months?

Gone are the hectic days of the weary;
she has returned to the carefree little dress
of the girl she longs to become again
let her skin bronze in midafternoon.

Hours pass as she fidgets on the steel
no book nearby nor any cell to distract her
from those precious moments spent with herself
her hand on her chest as she inhales softly.

It is difficult to find her peace yet
away from the cold walls of a dark office
too lonely with artificial air and dim lights
it is as if a rebirth for this child in a woman's flesh.

What does she wait for all this time
mesmerized it appears by her surroundings;
perhaps it is the answer to her daily dreams
a voice that speaks kindly through her private world.

Blood Of Ice

I know your blood is stone
crystals of ice in the summer sun
when the frigid blues scan the heavens
glass of mirrors to reflect your heart.

Still you sit pale as the past
a gentle breath barely escapes
from a heart-seeking life
your soul solid to all futures.

Life does not come easy this day
in this struggle to keep the world away
its hurts, its dangers, its hate
you remain prey, hidden to the foe.

See the pleasures of a welcomed guest
made of sun, light and warming touch
to soften those veins, and let it flow
the nectar of your noble dynasty.

I know your soul fears the crossing of
the threshold beyond the polar memories
leaving the swelling of frozen moments
for the burning of a passion yet unknown.

Your blood stops, facing the hated predator
to be unseen, cohorts of feeble babes
pretend to a lifeless existence so they may
escape in time, pleasure, and remain
in the certainty of their comfortable numbness.

Born At Last

Greetings to a world I abandon
for today I shed a strangest fate

Bewildered by the statue I contemplate
I have pondered enough with its parts.

Once I kicked a ball across a field
rolled in a warm mud to play a role
in this comedy of errors never rehearsed

Now I take the wrapping off to reveal a gift
a present so long kept a frigid secret
blue with the marks of a great many beatings.

The journey has endured
it is now time to consider a truth
beneath the pale shroud of this dawn.

There is no sense in the flesh
little credence to see in the bones
but a message read at last.

Greetings to a world I abandon
as it once wanted me to be.
as I now still could be

This new awakening as a birth
propelled by a twirling wave
I am free to become all and this I am.

A portrait in the hazy glass smiles
receptacle of mysteries answered
it is he and it is she, it is simply I.

Brain

It was a common day on the asphalt land
under neon lights, screaming rubber and
impatient humans of early years screeching.

Night and the tears of eternal heavens upon the path
he ventured carrying great joy under his arm
his soul glowing with the anticipation of his kin.

But he wandered into the jungle of man
surrounded by the machine of those who race
to no end chasing an existence never to be known.

There was a blunt echo in the fibers of the universe
his heart turned to dark as the gaiety he held fell
to the soiled surface of the dark map to nowhere.

Quiet soon returned to the theatre of his last instants
kind as he had been, he now lay in the puddle of his past
crimson of his hopes muddled with the gray of his spirit.

It had been a simple journey to another celebration
fireworks exploded all around in an explosion of death
and he dreamed far above the shattered remains of his life.

Breaking Another World

I broke the world with a word
and it lay there in pieces sad
tempted to cry, bleeding blue
poor little orphan planet.

I stood there with a twig and a lens
teasing rocks, mountains, and streams
for a single spark to ignite
that lonely heart defunct in space.

I felt bad, little giant under the stars
shards, slices, grains of dust
there was nothing left to do
but kick it under the clouds.

I broke another world with just a cry
it was fun at the time to see it collapse
like a butter cookie in little crumbs
jolly for a moment too brief.

Building A Wave

Singing a chord to another ear
stringing along on a mere dream
playing tug of war on the fault line
the void of the abyss, an attraction.

Pulling, hurting, hoping for a thread
a connection of touch, a deep sigh
relieved when the fall finally unites.

Climbing the steepest face, Mt Blanc
slipping, sliding, without safety.

Seeking the thin tether of birth,
unnatural perhaps, certainly desired,
for a flow to begin, blood, fluid,
purple with nobility, purity of Heaven.

Pointing to the other, the philosopher
thinks of mother, umbilical, so gentle,
a photograph lost at the bottom of his
memories, now so few, now so tame.

The symphony resonates to darkness,
unfathomed, in distances unknown,
deep inside, and yet, so near an origin.

A voice, a name murmured in timidity,
eyes closed, a wish uttered in silence
for a gentle pull from the new world,
approving welcome truly unrestrained.

Color Of Her Pain

What color would she paint her pain on a Friday night
as she sits patiently in wait of the coming hours?

What fabric would she choose for the somber evening
when the crowds pretend her invisibility once more?

Artist, she would choose the brushes of her dreams
and apply the watercolors on a standing canvas
to let the mixture of her tears cry to a floor of clouds.

No black, no white, but a rainbow of choices she never had
to taint the cotton candy of a youth so long captive
within the nebulous walls of those alien lives.

Her chest heaves once again, she sighs softly in her world
holding her soul so tight in a safer embrace, alone
she crosses her dreams over the bruised depth of her
a bluish aura of ice-cold memories envelops her future.

Shivering in the flesh she shares with her gentle kin
is there suddenly no hope for a warmer hearth?

Must she shed those moments endlessly again
Can she not rejoice in the reprieve of the gentle neighbor?

The shape of her pain grows into a mound of aching nectar
a strange substance bearing no semblance to her elegance
so close to grazing her satin sphere,
her disguised friend hopes
to simply shatter the opal treasure chest and free her.

Custom Made

Consider now that all of this was made for you
pores breathing life so the embrace continues
blood flows from rocks to rivers to oceans
and islands explode like so many supernovas.

Ponder upon the tower of skeletal structures
finding your way through the labyrinth of bones
a home built from dust to a glory yet to come
heaven in an uncertain valley of rugged storms.

Rest for a moment in the warmth of the flesh
fibers vibrate with the rhythm of the infinite song
pulses to the monument of memories to be
this refuge gapes its gates from the killing fields.

What indeed, if all of this was made just for you
a mass unrecognizable from the distance of loneliness
a size too large or too small in a moving present
freeze the instant, for this was made only for you.

Dreaming A Destiny

Down the valley, a torrent settles
into a glorious hollow but forgotten.

Peaks tower above the lush oasis
where sounds are muffled by peace.

A robe of dense foliage protects the grounds
jealous of its intimate treasures.

Winter slowly thaws into a renaissance
resurrecting the corpses of past promenades.

Suspended between wish and caress
the loving gaze looks upon a fertile world.

Years have molded the rugged lands
into the statuesque perfection of the muse.

Offering her safety to the seeking breast
she is still upon the earth of her womb.

Joyous songs now smile to the intruder
for he has earned a kiss and a touch.

Eternal Thread

The old piece of baling string for a belt,
the leftovers so he won't lose his old clogs.

And that's all he had and a dirty shirt,
with the worn-out pants soiled with grease.

Yet in there, somewhere, always he was
strong, ready for cuts, bruises, and pain.

The single string could have held the world one
as it kept his little universe from chaos.

He walked in the grooves of the earth,
mud on his shoes, limping in the sticky clay.

He dripped the sweat to feed the golden seed
looked down, looked up, and looked all around.

The crow let him go, the raven had yet eaten
the swallow never too slow, and the rain came.

He stopped for a moment, pain in the lower back,
straightened up, while the big sun threw a smile.

With his string in his hair, it was a calm moment,
perfect communion with the meaning he sought.

Final Leap

I will stand on the edge of the cliff in the high winds
venture to the brink of what may be crushing sand
tempted by the abyss deep under weakened skin.

'Tis better to take the long walk on the brittle bridge
visible to the one who seeks survival in every step
facing a void alone, with no arms to prevent the deadly fall.

The heart must become an icy stone of coal and sullen snow
pupils dilated in the darkness, salvation away from the light
courage pulled from energies seen to no other.

Floating liberated, denuded of all armors to evil and pain
helpless with no need to rely on an absent humanity
no harness will save from the conspiracy at play.

But the will itself, knowledge of all wisdom at hand
the body shed when the soul finds grandeur
gifted with flight I will stand on the edge of the ravine
and soar.

Flight Of The Hours

Time does not fly
unless perhaps it is written
on a paper airplane.

The dear treasure sits still
at attention as we walk by
feline in wait for another prey.

A two-legged creature uttered these words
today as night set upon his brow
heavy on the limbs, a globe ready to burst.

If the hours flew, we
would have to aim well
and take them down to the depths.

Were the seconds to rush
I think I might catch up and
reason with them.

But time does not fly child
perhaps you race to a death
and this one for sure, you will win.

Forever Ago

It has been ten minutes and a few decades
a wintery breeze short of a high plain tornado
at the bottom of a mountain mother of
Everest

Seconds ago, it was another century or perhaps
a millennium. Skies turned to strange hues of grey
swept by eternal torrents of watery air
the Pacific

Hands continue to mark daily routines
upon fiery entrails refusing to die
hesitating as a ghost attracted to the void
of Vesuvius.

Still now, sitting on an invisible throne
he contemplates a minute infinity
one and all within the final destination
in Space.

Gusts

I often wonder whence the power comes
giant hands caressing the limbs of my oaks
embraces to threaten their centuries.

It was but a moment when all was quiet
shadows spread across the countryside
deep with the balm of a new summer.

Where was this hurricane born
to what distances must I travel
and understand those origins?

Now all is calm at last and the storm has passed
I remain surrounded by the chill of a cloud
in awe at the power that again eluded my quest.

Half Past Life

It is late at life
days have gone to bed
under the shroud of light
left behind by a careless father.

A quarter of a time ago
blood flowed warm, thick
carrying a taste of iron and berries
now frozen in cracks in minimalistic crystals.

Too early into another month
the body refuses to chase a soul
emptier like the blinding hourglass
marbles drop in thunderous crashes.

Middle of nevermore thrice again
senses have parted ways onto the dial
making so many hands on the palm of eon
seconds, minutes, hours, and new dimensions.

Darkness is no longer
all stand still, in agony
she exhales her very last hopes
it is a moment past death.

Harvesting A Noble Death

Brushing the silk of corn
shining in the light
of a hot summer day.

Skin red with sun,
droplets running down
from under a timeless
blue Beret.

Leaving prints on the soil
he knew so well,
as if one, unified for eternity.

Lost in the midst
of the green giants,
naked skin cut by the sharp blades.

For a moment free,
only to be blinded by the golden glare,
a wave under the light breeze.

Towering atop the hill,
master of the Universe,
contemplating the valley where his river sings.

Eyes closed, a deep breath,
and it is all his
the world he knows.

Now one, they commune
and the land will give
so he may spread the wealth.

Another summer gone
fall and winter come;
you can rest cozy and warm;
we are safe.

His Daddy's Old Mirror

Sometimes he sheds a piece of his old chagrin
with a thought to the father of all his glee
the remembrance of a taste so long forgotten.

sometimes he looks into his daddy's old mirror.

Nothing has changed and he ponders why
there was a cake once, yesterday, or long ago
when he saw the dusk on a whole decade.
Why the excitement tingles deep within yet.

He knows he has dumbed many a blade
worn quite a few more of the working blues
scraped the skin, watched the clean blood pour
and see it come to life again, ten years old still.

He wonders now, alone in a world of close-knit kin
a child yet as he steps into his magic sled to the city
at the lady who time after time tenders a discount
to the one who giggles at the last trick played on his daddy.

Hissing Man

It smiles with bedroom eyes
hidden behind a curly fur
a soul hisses with each syllable.

The thing touches with pretended attention
holding a little too tight to the other
he takes possession of the innocent.

Hello, is said coated with thick honey
to soften the shell of the perceptive one
orbs piercing through the intimate garment.

What does it want so late in the season
when all has been laid on soft silk fabric
as it despairs of a table upon which to spread the bile.

In the strange shape of a half-finished human
it tries to spread a virus between its fangs
while at home it should be content with comfort.

But its hunger is insatiable with this soft sound
it wishes to seduce so it may lie better
and steal the lives from the kindhearted.

Free us from this evil with wooly mittens
for it is fire it spews beneath the skin
consumed by the very sin of the flesh.

Never satisfied with the granted gifts
it seeks to take all from those who suffer
glad to feed the pain only Satan ordains.

Holiday

Every day a holiday should you wish
yesterday a day for love or for hate
a fight broke out in the kitchen and
ended on a cold tile floor; no one died.

Remembering New Year's Day again,
already when the decade seems so old
whose year indeed?
whose birthday?
every day a holiday for her and a kiss.

There is no fourth of July to remember.

How About The Seasons

June may be my favorite month
after May
has ended of course.

May is not bad
endless as I wish it were
sweet
and so short all at once.

Famously reborn
rather than December
and of course, January
never to be seen again
created for the sake of life
October may otherwise
have the last word.

How Many Times...

By the altar they shed a tear
wondering how many times they must
throw their knees to the stone
as their hungry eyes cry to the storm.

Voices would delight in another scream
speaking words a hundred times rehearsed
beneath the sweet colors of millennial
stained glass made for the dreams of the meek.

Recalling verses of childhood's grand prayers
those pleading orbs raise to infinity
and ask why it must be so that they
return to the empty palace alone.

Their thoughts drift to other queries
as dreamy humanoid shapes waltz nearby
oblivious to the soft whispers of the souls
abandoned in a desert land of no one's making.

How many times must they hope for just a moment
for the smile of a might-be stranger
a should be lover lost in a painful kingdom
safe in the realm of absolute loneliness.

I, The Madwoman

You see me in the greasy aisle
avoiding contact with the living.

You hear me on the avenue
escaping the giant at rush hour.

I speak inanities with a grin
dressed in my Sunday best.

You may cringe when I laugh
in the middle of disconnected syllables.

Of course, you laugh at my pirouette
as I dance in the crowded square.

You call me crazy at midday
for my lonesome dialogue.

Little do you know that it is a joke
I play on you as I truly live.

If

If I never see you on the common paths of man
I will draw an avenue in the sky of teals and stars
so you may find your way back to my chest of treasures.

If I cannot hear your song in the cacophony of the day
it is a symphony of twenty tones I will create for you
and you will drift away on the waves of infinity.

If I am too distant to discern the scent of your hair
alchemist, it is in the darkness of my dreams
that I will create the fragrance of your pure essence.

If I am not able to taste the sweet breath of those lips
it is in the red of berries where I will remember
the divine aroma of the adored beating vessel.

If my touch suddenly is to fail me in this tormented world
in a vision, my soul will make a statue to your image
of a warmest stone I will carve the eternal sculpture.

If I do.

In Black And White

The image, odd reflection on faded paper
of a somber gaze, on a day so young yet
November again, reminder of a birth,
just a toddler, still in monochrome habit.

The marketplace, desolate, near the sounds
of the same old merry-go-round, sad again
what are they thinking, these deep browns?
perhaps of the next snapshot a year too soon!

Seven against a gray wall, laughing at the world,
mirror of surroundings so long forgotten,
no color in this domain, no joy in the smile!
who were they seeing those eyes near tears?

Just black in a suit, and white in the heavens,
he seems to long for the days of freedom,
happiness in scenes of tones and scents,
where at last, he may dance into the dark.

In Search Of The Word

A conductor's apprentice he seeks the strings of the cosmos
plucking at the occasional
through leaves of his thoughts.

Dreaming of Chopin on a shore of pebbles
complex as the last snow
he gently taps an index as he searches for the black ivories.

Perhaps the rhythm of an Africa he lost long ago
will animate his soul
drumming through the spheres a message
sweet as a heavenly potion.

Breath fresh as a newborn's in the early morning dew
he calls to the depths of space with the melody of the reed.

Musician, he knows the immaterial orchestra
surrounds his presence
child in the first lessons of the metronome he remains silent.

Twirling drunken artist desperate for expression he stumbles
still and forever unable to capture in the air
a sound to make up a sign.

Jolly Monsters

How can you tell them apart in the halls
when they laugh and they hug and they cry
acting like they just came from a holy place.

They gather in the popular eating places
pray to praise for a meal another earned
with bloody sweat, pains like lightning.

It may be Sunday again, day of rest
to them each day is one of glee
as they watch the weary labor for a penny.

Gooey they drool over a fifty-dollar appetizer
offered by a well-meaning God of their design
heads bowed they repeat their rituals.

There is no need for apologies in their world
everything that comes to them is their due
might well be since they own the old suburbs.

As they leave the hall reserved for them
they clamor their love for Him and His for them
as if He only cared for those who amass gold and platinum.

Yes, they are jolly, these giants in perfect suits
it is certain that their love is grander than the poor's
for they can afford tombstones engraved in diamonds.

Just Like The Old Poet

Three lumps of flesh on the couple's private bench
a memorial park made for the forgotten.

Decay soon to commence in the brownish masses
with no one to notice the odious aroma.

Thankful is this traveler on a journey to the void
to know that little will remain of the oddity.

Perhaps a last vulture will feast and the would-be carcass
too thin even for the repast of night critters.

Somewhere in an estranged multitude
a two-room palace has fallen to crumbles.

Hovering upon the treetops above this lonely spectacle
a soul smiles, for no living creature will notice.

After all, they did not seem to share his tears
thus he knows it is better to never have been known.

The blink of a faint light has now faded
he leaves no pain behind for it is his alone for eternity.

Keep The Door Ajar

A storm rages on the other side of comfort
flashes of light streak through the zenith
hail plunders the fragile walls of her home
thunder rolls with the destructive strength of tsunamis.

She wants to know what awaits
in that world she barely knows
but for the tales of a distant mother
will the assaults upon her breast soon lessen?

Peeking through the minute gap upon the sill
her fingers venture to preserve a space
to keep a vigilant eye into what might be
discovering a spectacle of dangers and ecstasies.

Heavenly drops slowly run down her hand
to make her shiver with surprise and fear
her body to the door she cannot let go
unfamiliar with a land she has longed to encounter.

Drawn to this unknown she cannot find the strength
to let go of the great curiosity
the gate must remain ajar for better or worse
for she might miss her great entrance to her own life.

Larry

Earlier today I eavesdropped again
at the bakery, the grocery, the chancellery
in a line to no end, long as perhaps eternity
behind Mr. Smith, one of a billion.

He carried a collection of wrinkles on his shoulders
took one step at a time and then three back
on a leash the old hound in scabs followed
his belly scraping the pavement in iron sparks.

He had some story to tell, a sister to meet
somewhere on this side of the cemetery
she died you know, he clamored, no later than
well, maybe yesterday, perhaps yesteryear.

Larry, he said, was his name, poor Larry
Mary was gone, no one to talk about his pain
so he grumbled, and I played with my change,
reminded him of a song he said, now he forgot.

You're lucky he yapped, you are young, no aches
no pus, no limp, and you got money in your pocket
to remember the roses you once bought for her
you know, the girl you married, the mother of your boy.

Now I was praying for time to take a leap of faith
and move into another space, to get me out of this line
for I too was beginning to feel aches and pains, and tears
I was not quite ready to put on another decade or two.

Larry, good old Larry, looked at me with the glassy greens
that's all I have you know, that's all there is to remember
when your home is so close to a field of graves and losses
my treasure, my life, aches, pains, and tender sorrows.

Last Drink

He often sat by the dim light of his dying days
empty cans littering a Persian spotted by tears
fingers stained by another addiction.

Struggling to alight the nicotine fix
eyes glued to the screen where words dance
he takes another long sip of bubbly yeasts.

He has retired from the common paths
his voice silent to mundane conversations
and seeks contact with a world beyond language.

Lost in a city where all fulfill a traced destiny
he finds no place inside conference rooms
assembly lines and cubicles that resemble home.

But his refuge is of strange molasses
blood mixed of tar and cheap potions
a poison he takes so he may live or he may die.

Landscapes desperate to come to life
beg for him to stay and love them still
as he cries in an agony beyond our grasp.

Today he is gone, this young soul of fifty
drowned in a river of unending sadness
his eyes closed on the dreams he did write.

Left Behind

Take the happiness with you
I will stay behind and take care of
the mope.

After all, many a tear will be shed,
no reason to take a chance for others,
they may slip, slide, break away forever,
unknowing of a drama so recent.

Take the happiness with you slowly,
for the pain will linger, it does always,
on the cold walls of light hues.

Let the glow of your supple warmth
last just a little longer for the frigid heart,
to thaw for a moment, to hope for an eon.

Remember to stay again; anticipation
of your return, no one will be aware
this intimate secret of two souls, ours alone.

Leaning on the heavy groan of cries, longings,
and heavy sighs, I promise to remain alert,
protect, cherish, and nurture what you leave,
to be safe in hands trembling of simple want.

Letter To My Brain

I do believe I was once quite insane,
and perhaps yet again from time to time
for I do count the needles on the pine,
I do stare at the rays of the stars.

In years of many months, I rely on heat,
relish in the cold, and seek the tempest,
in the morning glory of sweetest fogs
wishing a squirrel, I could frolic for acorns.

Swimming among the blades of grass,
I commune with the worm as he smiles to the Earth,
my body enrobed in a shroud of silk and life
sparks flash as I turn to the azure skies.

It is certain that once, too many a time, and again
I played with the marbles won from friends
of rainbows, crystal, ice and diamonds, only
to lose them and find myself without a home.

No doubt, in that which may have been a mind,
that this soul found boundless joy in its freedom
to run, to soar, to fall, and yet bounce once more,
under the gazes of a great many incredulous eyes.

Waves of an enchanted ocean taken by a hurricane
nothing can ever match the changes in this life
insanity yes, but so comfortable, so potent,
that it has borne more infants to the winds.

I do believe I was once blessed with insanity,
so this day, to seek it anew, I offer myself whole
to the lightning of the tornado, so I may be lifted
into ethers where all languages speak in the instant.

From time to time and sadly, also I cease my plays,
and morose, crushed by the weight of a million years,
I impatiently await another flight, for, sane, grounded
I know the answer lies elsewhere.

The race takes these aching remains through the forest
where bruises, cuts, and incessant assaults
insane yes, pained of course, nonetheless fulfilled
for now, the universe entire knows me.

Limbs And More

It is very hard to get used to
a mass of cells, flesh, blood in veins
to live inside, prisoner, well-being.

There, a leg I am told, with foot and toes
up above, the arm, left or right no matter
so many parts, moving, smooth for now.

In the penthouse at top, quiet, calm, awe
fear of heights, and motion sickness
decisions must be made to keep ahead.

There are others nearby, very much like me
I think that I think so that I am me at all
but you too, believe you are so.

Could we exchange these parts, hard, soft
silly, and find something different between
you, me, him over there, and she, right behind.

So odd, so hard to be one, to be self, to be me
if I move closer could I be you, my dear, for now
for an instant, a minute, a decade, forever perhaps?

Just a thought, let us close our eyes, yours, mine
forget these arms, legs, and the rest of it
and sleep, at peace, and meet again in our dreams.

Listen To The World Cry

I heard a synthesized cacophony
as I continued on the forest path
it screamed of pain and ire.

There was no source to be found
just echoes of reprocessed symphonies
mirrored on the bark of ancient oaks.

Footsteps accorded to the rhythm
vibrated through the core of nature
while all that should be, remained numbed.

I attempted another stroll through the city
surrounded by armies of my kin
their skin gray beneath glassy glances.

All hid within a space made to their moods
oblivious to what marvels may happen then
as they avoided contact with the essence of others.

I imagined all the songs ever conceived
blaring at grand speed through the waves
and stopped in my tracks to hear the world cry.

I may have been alone in Times Square
enveloped in a multitude of passing clones
listening to them deaf to this world.

Long Beards And Fat Bellies

He was spotted spinning the wheels of his
diesel guzzling the oil not even
the magnates could send his way fast enough.

It was at the local store where a regular
he walked away with the daily case
of the brew that generously nourished his entrails.

Cheetos from an ongoing night still adorned
the ancestral forest of grey overgrowth
he boasted as he ambled across the concrete.

Upon the gun rack the loaded rifle waited
for the first opportunity to rattle at a crowd
in the name of a fantasy he made up.

On the passenger seat lay the cornucopia
of words and verses and hymns and psalms
he continued to twist to his purpose.

In a few minutes in the grease-stained T
ornate with the precious fish
he was to declaim again the same directives.

His wife at the keyboard revered her
rhinestone dress as she sang mocked
by the luscious girlfriends in the congregation.

He told them all how to live, whom to hate
what not to read, not to watch R-rated films
while his soul traveled to climes of cherished depravity.

White hair, a beer gut to brave a grizzly
and the sacred text they all swear by
while the God they worship looks down in horror.

They fly hate flags through town
discard those who want to truly believe
and proclaim only they know any truth at all.

Loud Secrets

Two to speak loud and clear for all and too many to hear
secrets of an alcove and two more join for some chatter
it is a talk show of shaky lives, with no hope for redemption.

Their stay is brief, as their story is but a mere summary
of fantasies, tales shared without concern for safety
relieved by the gang of all sizes and generations
who take their spots, still warm, of their cold presence.

There they build substitutes for lives not begun,
illusion of mirages
splattering paragraphs with no rhyme
upon the walls all around
absent souls in shells of bodies
echoing of hollow words
clamoring of laughter, anger, gossip,
and shallow harmony.

Others will come, telling of the same romance
for the unmoved ears
until doors shut, night falls, silence overtakes
the strange arena
of a theater where reality remains scarce
and death prevails.

Macaroni And Apple Sauce

Six on that old clock and life is dark
streets almost dead so soon
but the home of stone shines.

It is a known ritual for the boy
a townie for his school days
no need for a bleak cafeteria.

The room is small, the table rustic
the lady still tresses her hair into a bun
grey for the decades galloping away.

There is no slim plasma on the wall
no song born of a mysterious device
just the crackling of a log in the stove.

She does not know central heating nor air
but a warm bed with heating stones
and a thick blanket for a cold night.

She is the great chef never forgotten
laboring for centuries in her house
always ready with the unlikely delights.

Macaroni baked topped in apple sauce
freshly caught sardines grilled on the live fire
and a dreamy kiss at bedtime.

Making Your Dream

Arthur lives in the forest next door
at the end of the street you walked last year
giddy girl when mother called you home!

It does not matter that Guinevere awaits his return
he is yours now as you run graceful to the mist
uncanny world of mystery in middle-aged times.

Darkness prevails in the early hours of a new day
chilled to your breast your red dress floats
sprinkled with the golden dust stars gifted to you.

Queen, king, knight, and squires have laid their weapons
by the foot of a common bed where life begins
you rest your soul on hands joined in prayer.

What are your hopes for the day you aim to delay
have you dreamed your last before reality settles
will you, at last escape in your intimate kingdom?

It seems another reaches to the kind heart
only to transgress into an impossible transcendence
illusion soon to vanish again within the desperate wish.

Meaning

What can the oak say to the wanderer of
that which it sees through the tears of the sun?

Can the grass raise its voice to such a pitch
so it may be heard by the unsolicited step?

What response will the air around formulate
to the uncertain motion of the disturbing shape?

Will the critters of so many kinds raise legs and paws
to warn their kin of the doom upcoming?

Where will he go, unaware of his deeds' doings
to compose a portrait when the mirror remains of stone?

Will he simply lay his old hopes down on the straw bed
and forget alone that this life of his, too has a meaning?

Memories For The Otherworld

We commit moments to posterity
to be told in ink on decaying parchment.

Tales of a thousand and ten lives
written on the in-folios of the temple.

Chattering voices cover the peace
in an eternity we hope to unravel.

What will you and I recall of this citadel
where we still share the intimacy of the pure?

I know every curve of your delights
the tremors of your heart as you savor the hour.

Your essence reverberates to eternal distances
entangled with the fibers of our destinies.

You laugh in the corner of the alcove
invisible to the eye, so solid to the spirit.

Seeking the light beyond the horizon
we search for tomorrow's memory.

What history will we take with us to fancy
the closeness we made under the stormy mobs?

For now, we rest in the warmth of a secret hearth
dreaming a single kingdom atop the safety of Olympus.

Missing

A string broke on the old acoustic
neck splintered near the last fret
sounds transport him to nowhere
a ghostlike image reflected onto the body.

A muscle spasm awoke him at midnight
dreadful silence surrounded the land
jerked by thin tensions in the air
he felt the weight of death on his chest.

The smell of fresh pine hovered
transported to a time long gone
they sighed as they looked to the horizon
a scent of insignificant deaths upon their souls.

Hours or perhaps decades since this void
dug a deep abyss on a path to bliss
what may she think in her dangerous abode
missing the knight she never really saw?

Mother

In wonderment, I devour the photo
a distant memory I can not share
a life had been made, she held it.

Two eyes closed in full rest, after
the ordeal of their birth, to a new
world, unexplored, unknown.

Two eyes open, in the shape of suns
make contact with a stranger,
through years they never shared.

Madonna, she cradles her creation
bearing no crown, yet she is aglow
radiating with a million more sparks.

I long to partake in the intimacy
to find the opening in the clutch of
arms so eagerly tight through time.

Perhaps it will be the morrow, when
the image vibrates into another pose
and a stranger is allowed to join the union.

My Girl

My girl, she dances in the room
while I work, my girl Julie
gorgeous as she dances in the room.

My girl, she dances in the park
as I read yet another book
and she smiles as she dances in the park,
Sally.

My girl Amanda, she dances in my head
as I work on nothing but another dream
she smiles at me, my girl
and tomorrow she will dance in my kitchen
as I sip on a brand-new day.

My girl, she floats in my life
unreal as I walk down the hall
to another novel, another biography
she seems a little sad, my girl Sabrina
as I sit in my chair to open the book.

My girl, she dances between the pages
a little distracted
a little less light
a little less happy
she seems to disappear, as she dances away
my girl Sonja, trying to distract me
for just an instant.

My girl Zelda, she succeeded
for that one second as she danced with Isadora
just a few steps and tomorrow my girl
will dance in my room and I will read the book
dream my thoughts and a volume will come alive
for my girl, Savannah.

My Midas

Midas long before him touched them
all under his hand changed to gold
all was transformed to the highest
perhaps to satisfy and show what was sublime.

The knife, every day, used for lunch and work
a glass and a cup, for the much-enjoyed drinks
the spoon, and the fork that knew him so well
felt a heart and soul that made them precious gems.

By the shed, the axe's handle still warm
all his garden tools, many forever resting
to him a room, his sunroom, his museum
where so often he shelled the nuts harvested.

His favorite chair now retired to the attic
silence prevails where the four wheels used to hum
prints in the muddy soil like a dinosaur's foot
still resounding with the care he took.

Resting for just an instant, on the pillar of the barn he built
ready to exert his strength again on a world awaiting him
the atmosphere even retains the glorious shape of his life
with hand and foot, all of his humanly being.

Wrinkle or sweet caress on the smooth surface of time
recalling his passage, it has changed to never return
to the form which it showed before, like Midas
he came and left his mark, indeed he did.

My Rolls And I

My Rolls and I, we have crossed the country
on broad tires and great meals
why not splurge when you can travel
in the plush seats of a British giant.

We found the 100-foot yacht anchored
in the Frisco Bay shining with silvery glances
the envy of all those foreign passers-by
Americans are so rich and lucky they say.

It was to be a journey around the world
with captain, servants in white and blue
a virtuoso chef in his artist laboratory
not to forget the media room down below.

Stops in every port to tan by the Hilton
savor delicacies only available
in restaurants with limitless stars
and purchase proof of our passage in gold.

Never Too Late

It will never be too late to kick the can
perhaps left in the last glimmer of hope
for the old man on his shiny wheels.

It is not too late gentle matriarch to jump rope
as you gaze through the shady glass
in a jungle you once so nurtured.

There is still time to look to the mirror
to speak with that soul you know so well
before you surrender to eternal dreams

You know you can again sing that tune
with your broken voice into the breeze
for those lips continue to murmur a life.

Smile o my father my, friend, my everyone
your teeth shine with the kindness of ages
shaken by the struggles of so many days.

Love as if you courted with your teens
suffer the hurt of another oblivious heart
and cry with the joy of loving for the first time

It is not too late to become you in the dawn
you may leave us in the cold of another morrow
but you will still wear that girly dress.

Brave the hours with your last breaths
run, take flight against the broken bones
you can yet, my kind kin, be a child.

Nice Piece Of Living

Clipping discounts in the Sunday rag, a habit
once a pastime before the big game
now a goal to fill a gaping photo album.

Pounds of news used to be a pleasure
shared one section at a time with a lover
now a doorstop to keep winter ices away.

He remembers the funnies in technicolor
syndicated laughter for a whole planet
when family played rock scissor paper.

The endless sports pages of local glories
animated their eyes before the giant pizza pie,
rot forgotten beneath the front porch.

Yellowed-out parchment a sad duplicate of his flesh
they are a meek portrait of who he once was
jolly in the privacy of simple weekly pleasures.

Lucky for him he can still find deals for his needs
eager as he awakes to rummage the endless ads
last dim remnant of a joyful glitter in his soul.

No More Decembers

September
you could have waited for another
December
your birthday was up, another year vanished.

But it had to be your way with the anger.

I knew you once, in the fields of corn
the white walls of a birthing home
among the stones of tombs to be
yours there, gaping at ready.

Raging
in the fire of these girls you loved
screaming
at the colors you refused to hear.

Poor kid, you lost your language then.

What feelings hover over what you left behind
smiles of ancestors who still wonder
and a sterile piece with vague words
not a thought on the tile of raspberry cream.

So still
little boy running around the table with a flask
far gone
young man filled with the bile of hating headlines.

Book closed now, heavy with lead, empty of memories.

You had your last cocoa on the weekend leave
hair cut for the crew, dreaming of a favored drug
it was not you there across the aluminum table
a ghost in the making, your victory in waiting.

The Death Of Summer

They go to camp because that's what they do
under orders from the leaders of the group
smiling they board the rusty yellow bus
soon to be retired for prison transport.

They pretend to be grateful for the adventure
bags full of new Nikes, the latest video game
and their favorite bar of fruit and candy
departing they cry for their empty dens.

This night they will sit by a fire beneath the trees
a circle of temporary friendships for a lifetime
sing a few songs, make the infamous s'mores
and go to sleep crying over a sight of home.

The week will unravel with well-intentioned fun
designed by those so close to them they may care
for another record of a perfect summer
anonymous good times of a military platoon.

The good-byes will come soon enough
they will hug, they will cry, they will laugh
promises made never to be fulfilled
beyond the gates of the new school year.

Trashing The World

Sitting behind the steel wheel of his mean machine
deafened by the invading sounds of an impossible chant
the uneven incisors plowing through an apparent meal
oozing with unnatural grease.

A garland of melted yellow paste adorns the facial hair
while fat lips suck energy from a plastic tube
gas emerges from the flabby flesh
satisfied the creature litters the forest and drives off.

Another recently freed into adulthood
reclines on the balcony of his new prison
it was time to celebrate nothing once again
from a fourth story anything can happen.

Learners of physics and other matters
test the ability of a commode to take flight
admire the shattering of a dresser no longer to their fancy.
smithereens like confetti on a national holiday.

They laugh and they scream and ridicule
a world they would not want for their own
a trash heap made of their many heartless souls
memories of a futureless race.

Where have all the good kids gone
parentless aberrations of a depraved age
asks the burgeoning poet as she tries to find a path
through what was the land of her careful dreams.

If This Is Where God Lives...

If this is where God lives
he must be mighty cold
surrounded by frozen hearts
false prophets and Bible thumpers.

If God lived here, he would wonder
where did the love go, he made of eternal sands
laboring as he fashioned all creatures
with flesh, blood, and saintly sweat.

If God happened to need a place to stay
whose hearth would he choose
when none is worthy of His greatness
even upon the great hills of our country.

Perhaps He will pay us a visit soon
and right the wrongs of men in dark suits
adorned with neckties and golden bracelets
as they preach a Word invented by greed.

But this is not where God lives
for he has been disowned in his own land
relegated to the outskirts of the expanse
by would-be black robes and their modern inquisition.

$200 A Night

Who knew
you could rent a palace
for a mere 200 quid
and get a whole night
settle in at 3 in the afternoon
be gone by 11 the next day
refreshed in thousand dollars sheets
ten-dollar diet cokes
thirty-dollar hamburgers
and a loaded mini bar.

What a deal
for everyone of course
to stay within walls of marble
glistening with diamonds and gold
ornate with a giant plasma screen
one million channels no one watches
and a luxurious beach ten stories below
but the pool sounds better in its garden
near equipment to shed pizzas and sweets
away from the hot air of an August eve.

Why bother
with the streets like a museum
when you spend a thousand dollars
on a suite near the Champs-Elysées
your Bentley parked by security guards
armed to the teeth to make your vacation
a restful paradise on a king-size bed
you might attend a show yet again
the food is so very fine when delivered
by a bellboy in Renaissance livery.

Meanwhile she camps
atop the lush meadows of the Rockies
13,000 feet closer to heaven
alone with the elusive creature of the wild
cans of beans her only repast for weeks

beautiful under the stars her accomplices
her face projects an incomparable glee
filled with a life so few will achieve
in their million-dollar cocoons
so far below they may not even exist.

In The Ivory Tower

A fortress built upon a medieval mound
the adventurer may guess its towers behind the fog
of an old Scottish moat and its granite barricades.

The drawbridge smells of musty oak
its chains rusted halfway between New Year's and
an age when the visitor still came to hear the Knight's tale.

The iron gate weighs with the centuries it knows
crushing a lock whose key has melted within the dreams
of the persistent explorer on his trusted steed.

But it is silence which the crow still writes onto the breeze
its wings taking a chance into the deserted court
where damsels once held a great feast for a lady.

Wondering what came of this gathering of pearls and rubies
while the hesitant squire dares not continue his quest
an unlikely groom centuries too late takes another step.

High above the clouds, a light flickers through the glass
he might have heard a call for mercy, a cry for grace
for there, she writes yet the life her innocence deserved.

His cape floats with the feeble breaths of her bosom
as he takes a knee in awe of the one who lives on
the treasure chest to remain a secret for eternity.

Old West Glories

'Will you be home tonight?' He asked.?
she could only shrug her weary shoulders.

Her mother, her grandmother too
walked in the snow barefoot, uphill both ways
for decades so they could share their kindness.

Now she drives the Chevy her father left her
braving construction and fiery storms
in the age of safety far from the war.

She still trembles with somber thoughts
of another day in the trenches of academe
without the duke's old, trusted six-shooter.

She recalls double features on steamy Sunday
Nights at the abandoned drive in
watching gunslingers at the Okay Corral.

Great days of carefree shakes and fries
when the only fighting they knew was so distant
now she is near tears before the school's concrete barricade.

The Duke laughed as he made the law
in an age when criminal hearts always failed
but things have changed as evil now seems a hobby.

Scanning the room full of petrified smiles
she wishes she could crack a little humor
but it is too late in such a decadent age.

No one knows who the next offender will be
standing at attention until the end of recess.

If The Noise Could Cease

They might be in a race for their lives
roaring up the curvy road to the top
all wildlife making way in a cloud
of dusty memories and unlikely futures.

Screams of metal and rubber remain
suspended in air unwilling to settle
the trace these strange creatures
will cast behind, noise upon a symphony.

Leaving the carcasses of steel and rust
the journey continues into their obscure world
down musty corridors into echoing cells
where the clamors will persist into dawn.

They may not wait until morning to resume
the strange poundings in the air
voices raised to break the atmosphere
just to be lost in a haze of oblivion.

Far from them, peace in the meadow
a realm apart from those useless creatures
bolstering successes they never knew
and quiet at last for those who want to listen.

Spitting In The Grass

How elegant she thought to see the teen spit
a substance of yellowish paste and pus
into the carefully groomed Bermuda of the great mansion.

How satisfying it must be for the man of forty
teeth dark with a brief high, fingers dripping
with a yellowish oil
to prepare for such a divine enterprise.

A shirt spotted with stained circles testifies
to the supreme gentlemanly manners of the creature
as he awaits by the doors of the castle
to allow for his triumph.

What a view it is to ponder this Sasquatch
dripping with the remains of a meal of grease and blood
attempting to comprehend the battles of the South.

The abundant brood follows imitating the gargantuan
distant his mirror image in the shape of a wife
assassinates a Marlboro in the gravel of the estate.

Soon again they will sit on their welfare porch
guzzling cheap beer courtesy of a bewildered Sam
and share the horrors of their ineptness
with chain-smoking neighbors.

Almost asleep on the swing my girl softly sobs
looking for the beauty buried under the rubble
of billions who left their souls in some gas station toilet.

I will hold her for ages into our deaths
so we may live in the sublime
forevermore.

The Proposal

He set one knee to the ground
as his elders once insisted
every day as if rehearsing a future.

Facing all cardinal points in his quest
trusting the fibers of the universe
to speak for him to the coveted soul.

I saw him once atop an isolated tower
he had built with the labors of his words
arms extended in prayer but also in submission.

He seemed to plead for the same fancy
his gaze to the heavens all around
her image upon the blue of the skies.

Proposing a pure alliance to her
he wondered whether she might hear
as his breath cried a most pleasurable agony.

www.ingramcontent.com/pod-product-compliance
Lightning Source LLC
Chambersburg PA
CBHW071317080526
44587CB00018B/3255